Favorite Songs of Praise

Solos, Duets, Trios with Optional Piano Accompaniment

Arranged by Michael Lawrence

CONTENTS

© 2009 Alfred Music Publishing Co., Inc.
All Rights Reserved. Printed in USA.

ISBN-10: 0-7390-6657-9
ISBN-13: 978-0-7390-6657-7

Cover photo courtesy of Bill Davenport

ABOVE ALL

TENOR SAXOPHONE

Words and Music by
PAUL BALOCHE and LENNY LEBLANC
Arranged by MICHAEL LAWRENCE

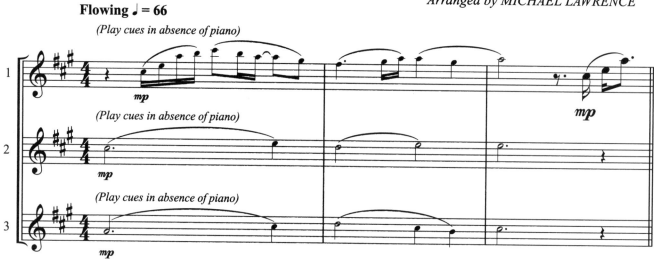

BLESSED BE YOUR NAME

Words and Music by
BETH REDMAN and MATT REDMAN
Arranged by MICHAEL LAWRENCE

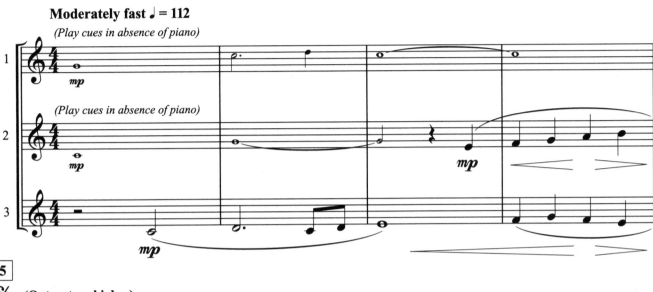

COME, NOW IS THE TIME TO WORSHIP

Words and Music by
BRIAN DOERKSEN
Arranged by MICHAEL LAWRENCE

DRAW ME CLOSE

Words and Music by
KELLY CARPENTER
Arranged by MICHAEL LAWRENCE

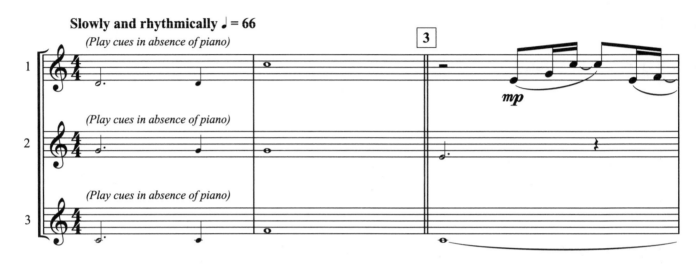

(Play cues in absence of piano)

(Play cues in absence of piano)

(Play cues in absence of piano)

(Play cues in absence of piano)

14

HERE I AM TO WORSHIP
(LIGHT OF THE WORLD)

Words and Music by
TIM HUGHES
Arranged by MICHAEL LAWRENCE

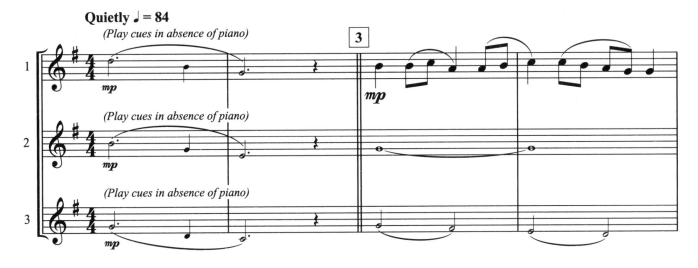

HOW DEEP THE FATHER'S LOVE FOR US

Words and Music by
STUART TOWNEND
Arranged by MICHAEL LAWRENCE

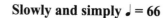

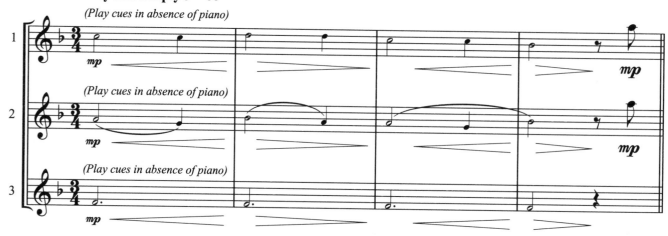

HOW GREAT IS OUR GOD

Words and Music by
JESSE REEVES, CHRIS TOMLIN and ED CASH
Arranged by MICHAEL LAWRENCE

I COULD SING OF YOUR LOVE FOREVER

Words and Music by
MARTIN SMITH
Arranged by MICHAEL LAWRENCE

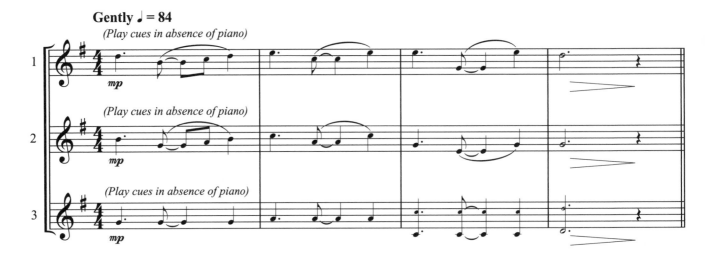

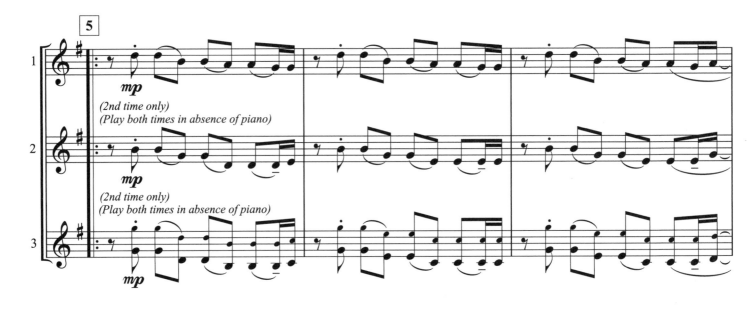

IN CHRIST ALONE
(MY HOPE IS FOUND)

Words and Music by
STUART TOWNEND and KEITH GETTY
Arranged by MICHAEL LAWRENCE

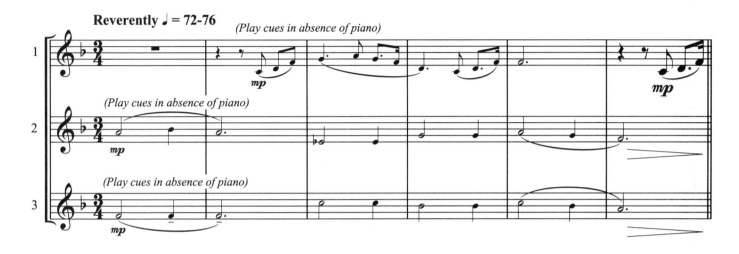

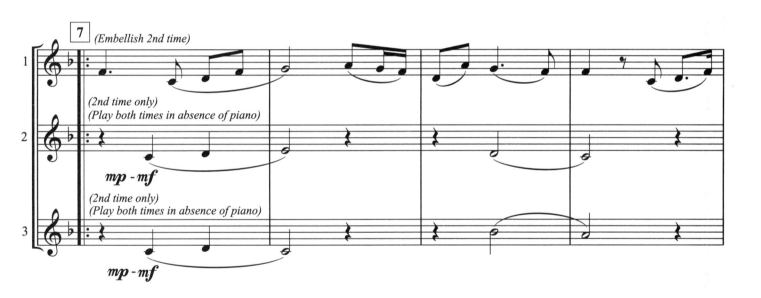

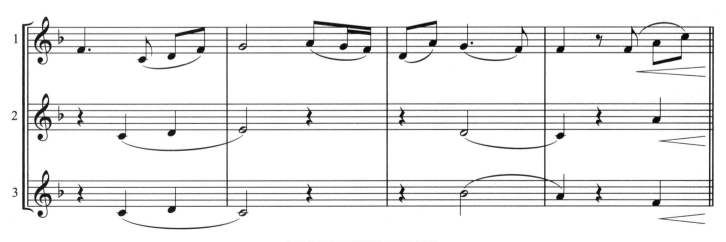

LORD I LIFT YOUR NAME ON HIGH

Words and Music by
RICK FOUNDS
Arranged by MICHAEL LAWRENCE

MY SAVIOR, MY GOD

Words and Music by
AARON SHUST
Arranged by MICHAEL LAWRENCE

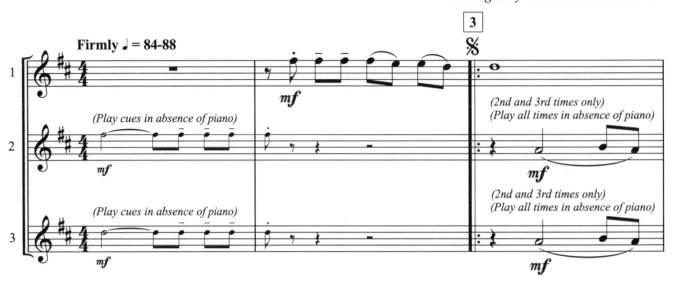

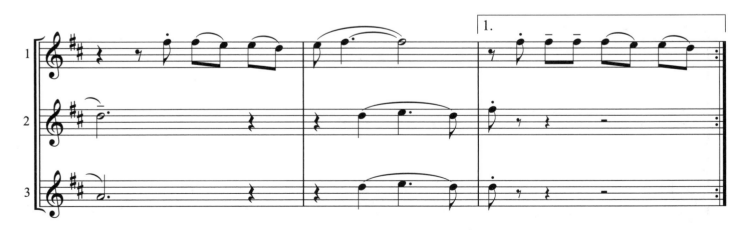

2nd time To Coda ⊕

D.S. 𝄌 al Coda

⊕ Coda

THERE IS A REDEEMER

Words and Music by
MELODY GREEN
Arranged by MICHAEL LAWRENCE

36

32734

THERE IS A REDEEMER

Words and Music by
MELODY GREEN

Arranged by MICHAEL LAWRENCE

32734